Bedtime on the Farm

by Alex Eeles

illustrated by Davide Ortu

CAMBRIDGE UNIVERSITY PRESS

UCL Institute of Education

On the farm, it is time for bed.

'I will go and get the animals,' says Dev.

'But where are they?'

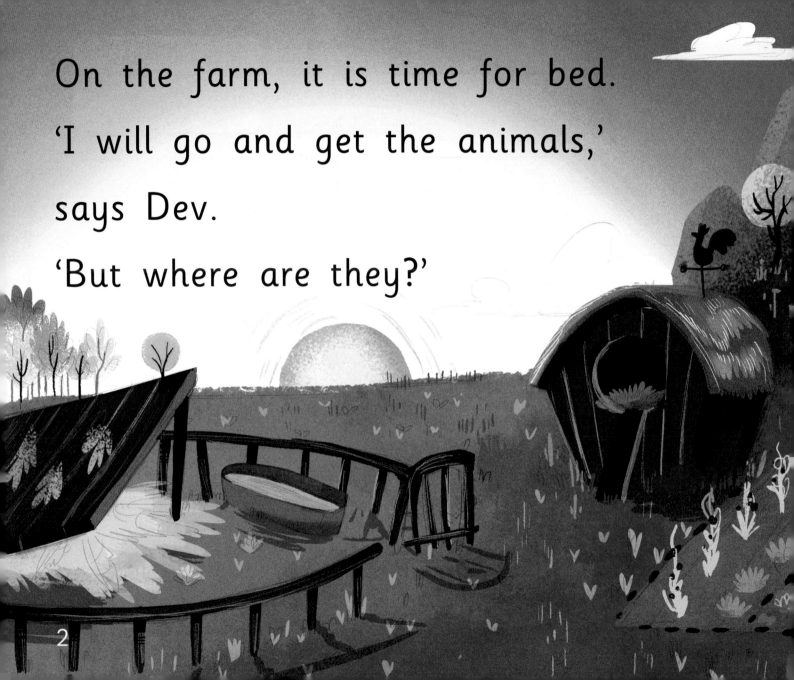

Cow will not go to bed.

'Come on, Cow,' says Dev.

'Here is some grass for you.'

'Time for bed,' says Dev.

Goat will not go to bed.

'Come on, Goat,' says Dev.

'Here is an apple for you.'

'Time for bed, Goat,' says Dev.

The hens will not go to bed.

'Come on, hens,' says Dev.

'Here is some corn for you.'

'Time for bed,' he says.

On the farm, all the animals
are in bed.

'Goodnight, everyone!' says Dev.

Bedtime on the Farm Alex Eeles

Teaching notes written by Sue Bodman and Glen Franklin

Using this book

Developing reading comprehension

On the farm, Dev wants to put the animals to bed. But they need persuading. Strong support from the illustrations provides good opportunities to begin to call for phrased reading.

Grammar and sentence structure

- The repetition of sentences and phrases across up to four lines of text consolidates one-to-one correspondence and return sweep.
- Begin to read smoothly and using a finger to track at points of difficulty only.
- The use of *'says'* may be unfamiliar to many children, and needs supporting prior to reading.

Word meaning and spelling

- Opportunity to rehearse and read a wide range of known high frequency words.
- Practise and consolidation of regular decodable words.

Curriculum links

Maths – This story shows a night-time routine on the farm. Children could discuss the tasks that need doing on a farm and sort them into Day/Night or to extend the level of challenge, Morning/Afternoon/Evening and Night. Links could be made with other time-sequenced stories.

PSHE – Dev looks after the animals on the farm. What do the children do to look after animals in their homes and communities? 'Looking after Animals' (Pink B band) could be reread to add to this discussion.

Learning Outcomes

Children can:

- use punctuation to inform phrasing and expression
- use phonic knowledge to solve new and novel words
- comment on the events and characters in the story, making links to other stories.

A guided reading lesson

Book Introduction

Give each child a book and read the title to them.

Orientation

Give a brief overview of the book, using the verb in the same form as it is in text.

Dev is putting the animals to bed. But they don't want to go.

Preparation

Page 2: Ask the children to locate all the places that the animals live. Ask the children to suggest what animal might live there. Draw out the names of the animals in the book, supporting where necessary.

Tell the children that the farmer in the story is called Dev – ask them to say his name slowly and find the word in the text, running their finger under it from left to right to check that they have found the word that looks right.

Rehearse the longer sentence *'I will go and get the animals.'* by reading it aloud and asking the children to follow each words as you read. Then ask them to practise reading it. Repeat with *'But where are they?'*, also noticing the question mark. Rehearse saying the question as a smooth phrase and with expression.

Page 4: Say: *Oh no! Cow will not go to bed? Why do you think that is?* Take some responses from the children. Draw their attention to the illustration of Dev